T0379164

THE AMAZING HUMAN BODY

THE HUMAN
CIRCULATORY SYSTEM

by Chelsea Xie

BrightPoint Press

San Diego, CA

© 2025 BrightPoint Press

an imprint of ReferencePoint Press, Inc.

Printed in the United States

For more information, contact:

BrightPoint Press

PO Box 27779

San Diego, CA 92198

www.BrightPointPress.com

LIBRARY OF CONGRESS CATALOGING-IN-PUBLICATION DATA

Name: Xie, Chelsea, author.
Title: The human circulatory system / by Chelsea Xie.
Description: San Diego, CA: BrightPoint Press, 2025 | Series: The amazing human body | Audience: Grade 7 to 9 | Includes bibliographical references and index.
Identifiers: ISBN: 9781678209681 (hardcover) | ISBN: 9781678209698 (eBook)
The complete Library of Congress record is available at www.loc.gov.

CONTENTS

AT A GLANCE

- The heart, blood, and blood vessels make up the circulatory system.

- The circulatory system delivers oxygen and nutrients throughout the body. It also removes waste, such as carbon dioxide, from cells and organs.

- Blood is made up of red blood cells, white blood cells, and platelets. Blood also includes a fluid called plasma.

- There are three types of blood vessels. They are arteries, veins, and capillaries.

- The heart pumps blood throughout the body. Blood flows in one direction through the heart.

- Conditions that affect the circulatory system include coronary artery disease, heart attacks, and strokes.

- Some conditions that affect the circulatory system are present at birth. Heart defects are one example.

- People can take steps to keep the circulatory system healthy. Adopting a healthy diet, exercising regularly, and managing stress can benefit the circulatory system.

LISTENING TO THE HEART

It was an ordinary winter day. Claudia was walking her dogs. She had walked about 2 miles (3 km) without any issues. But then she began to feel that something was wrong. She felt lightheaded. She also felt short of breath. It almost felt like a panic attack. But this was something new.

Claudia immediately thought about her heart. Her family had a history of heart problems. She called her doctor. The doctor

Cold weather can put extra strain on the heart by narrowing the blood vessels. This can raise the risk of heart attacks.

Emergency rooms are hospital departments that treat sudden, life-threatening medical conditions.

told Claudia to go to the emergency room (ER).

Doctors in the ER checked Claudia's blood pressure and heart rate. Both were very high. But they did not find anything wrong with Claudia's heart. She did not have pain in her chest or arms. These are the most common signs of a heart attack.

However, Claudia continued to worry about her heart. Her anxiety stopped her from doing daily activities. She no longer went on long walks with her dogs. She avoided driving.

Claudia went to a **cardiologist**. The doctor recommended cardiac rehab. This program is designed to improve heart health. Part of the program includes supervised exercise. Claudia suddenly became very tired during one of the exercise sessions. She felt a heavy pressure on her chest. She was taken to the ER. The doctors ran a test on her. It confirmed she was having a heart attack.

Claudia had life-saving heart surgery. She fully recovered. Claudia began to share her story with others. She wanted people

The body's systems are interconnected. Each system relies on and supports the others.

to know the importance of listening to their bodies.

CIRCULATORY SYSTEM BASICS

A heart attack is one thing that can go wrong with the circulatory system. This body system includes the heart, blood, and blood vessels. It delivers oxygen and nutrients throughout the body. It also helps remove waste.

Problems with the circulatory system can be deadly. **Organs** in the human body need oxygen to work. Other body systems shut down if the circulatory system cannot deliver enough oxygen. Fortunately, people can take steps to keep this system healthy.

CHAPTER ONE

WHAT IS THE CIRCULATORY SYSTEM?

The circulatory system is the body's delivery system. Blood carries nutrients, oxygen, and other substances throughout the body. It also helps the body get rid of waste. Blood travels through the body in blood vessels. The heart beats to force blood through these vessels.

Most nutrients come from the food people eat. Nutrients include sugars, fats, and other substances. The body breaks

Some veins are visible under the surface of the skin. They may appear blue due to the way human skin filters light.

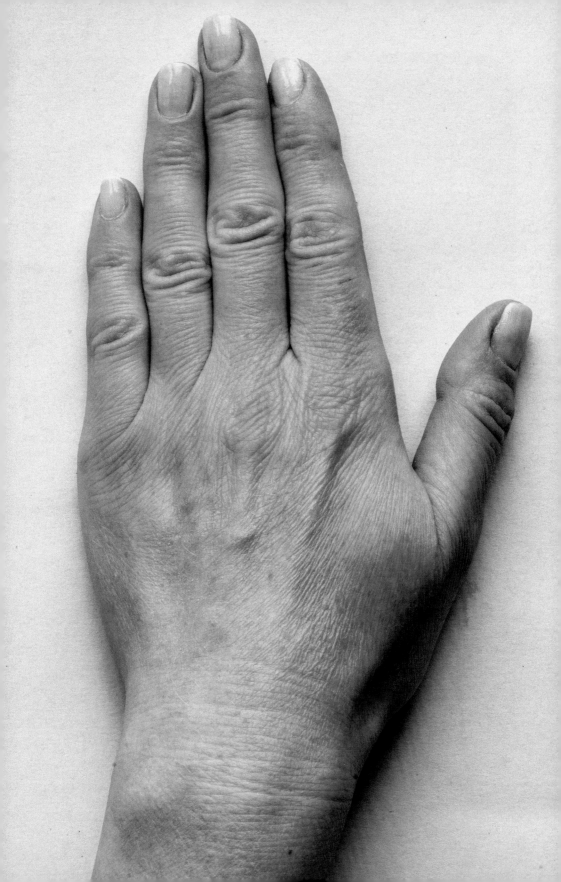

Parts of the body cannot go without oxygen for more than a few minutes. That's why people need to breathe continuously.

down food into nutrients during digestion. Nutrients provide energy. The body uses this energy to fuel itself. Dr. Lawrence Phillips describes the importance of blood in nutrition. "The tissues of the body need a constant supply of nutrition in order to be active," he says. "If [the heart] is not able to supply blood to the organs and tissues, they'll die."[1]

Almost all cells in the body also need a regular supply of oxygen. The circulatory system and **respiratory** system work together to make this happen. Blood vessels bring blood to the lungs. Blood cells enter the lungs carrying carbon dioxide. Cells in the body produce this waste gas. A build-up of carbon dioxide can harm the body. Blood exchanges carbon dioxide for oxygen in the lungs. The body then breathes out the carbon dioxide. Meanwhile, the blood carries oxygen to parts throughout the body.

Blood helps the body remove other kinds of waste as well. Many bodily processes produce waste. Some waste comes

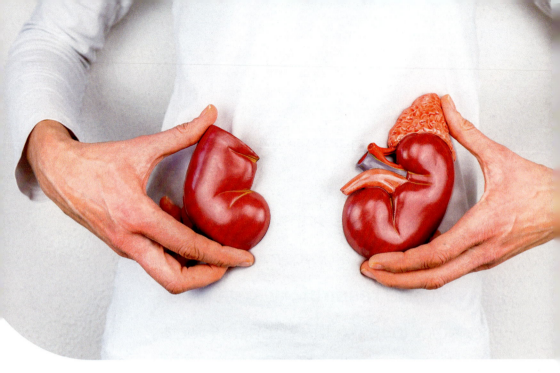

People normally have a pair of kidneys. They are located in the abdomen on each side of the spine.

from food. Blood carries waste to the kidneys. Blood also takes excess water to the kidneys. The kidneys filter the waste and water out of the blood. The body releases the waste and water as urine.

COMMUNICATION

The circulatory system allows distant body parts to communicate. Blood carries chemical messengers called hormones.

Hormones work like keys. They fit into specific receptors on cells throughout the body. Hormones trigger a response when they bind to a receptor.

Hormones allow the body to perform many complex processes. For example, **glands** near the kidneys release cortisol. This hormone plays a role in the body's response to stress. Blood carries cortisol throughout the body. It causes the liver to release a sugar called glucose. Glucose gives the body the energy it needs to react to stress. Cortisol also affects the brain. It raises alertness.

IMMUNE RESPONSES

The immune system protects the body from **germs** and other invaders. The circulatory system helps the immune system do its job. It does this by circulating white blood cells and other elements of the immune system.

White blood cells make up a small part of blood. But they play a big role in immune responses. There are several types of white blood cells. Some find and destroy germs. Others get rid of damaged cells in the body.

White blood cells flow through the bloodstream. They patrol the body. They alert the immune system of any dangers. These include signs of infection. The immune system sends a response through the blood to the site of the problem.

Antibodies are also part of the immune system. They are proteins found in the blood. Antibodies attach to invaders. This invites white blood cells to attack them.

Each antibody is unique to specific germs. When a new germ invades the body, the immune system creates antibodies that can deal with it. This allows the body to recognize the germ after the first infection. The body can then respond to the germ much faster in the future. This is why people can become immune to an illness after getting better.

How Much Blood Do People Have?

Blood makes up about 7 to 8 percent of a person's weight. That means the average adult has about 4.8 to 6 quarts (4.5 to 5.7 L) of blood. The amount of blood that a person has also depends on factors besides weight. These include sex and age.

CHAPTER TWO

HOW DOES THE CIRCULATORY SYSTEM WORK?

The parts of the circulatory system work together like a plumbing system. The heart is like the pump. It pushes blood through the system. The blood vessels are like the pipes. They connect the heart to muscles, tissues, and organs throughout the body.

Blood is made up of several parts. Most of blood does not consist of cells. About 55 percent of blood by volume is plasma.

Red blood cells beginning at the heart can move through the body and back to the heart in less than 1 minute.

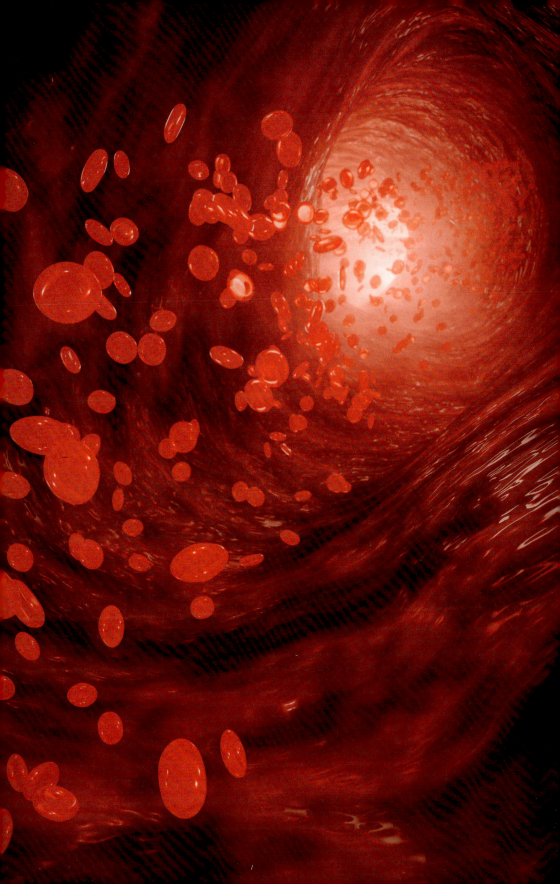

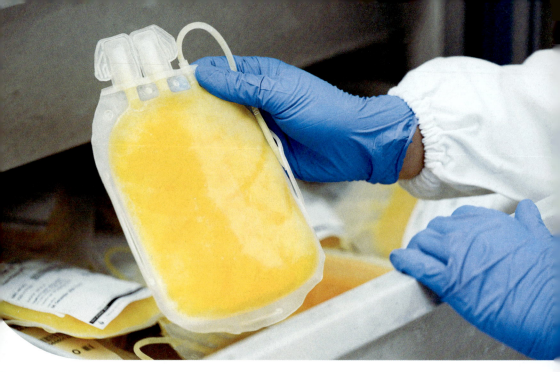

Blood plasma is typically yellow. This is due to the nutrients and substances it contains.

Plasma is a mixture of water and nutrients. It helps blood flow smoothly. It carries nutrients throughout the body. It also removes waste from cells and organs.

Red blood cells make up about 40 to 45 percent of blood. They are shaped like discs. Red blood cells are flexible. They can squeeze through narrow blood vessels. Red blood cells contain a special protein called hemoglobin. This protein allows red blood cells to carry oxygen. Hemoglobin contains iron. This gives blood its red color.

White blood cells make up about 1 percent of blood. These cells fight germs. They also play a role in allergic responses. And they help wounds heal.

Platelets are the smallest blood cells. They make up less than 1 percent of blood. Platelets help stop bleeding. Dr. Marlene Williams explains how this works. She says, "Platelets . . . bind together when they

Bone Marrow

Most blood cells are created in bone marrow. Bone marrow is the spongy center of bones. Blood cells become damaged over time. They need to be replaced. The body is constantly making new blood cells. It makes about 2 million new blood cells every second.

recognize damaged blood vessels."[2] This forms clots that prevent blood from escaping blood vessels.

BLOOD TYPES

Different people's blood cells vary in small ways. These differences allow people to divide blood into blood types. Blood types come from proteins called antigens. Antigens are on the surface of blood cells. They allow the immune system to tell which cells belong to the body. The immune system attacks cells that do not have the right antigens. This is why blood type matters when a person receives donated blood. People who have lost blood can replace it only with blood that works with their type.

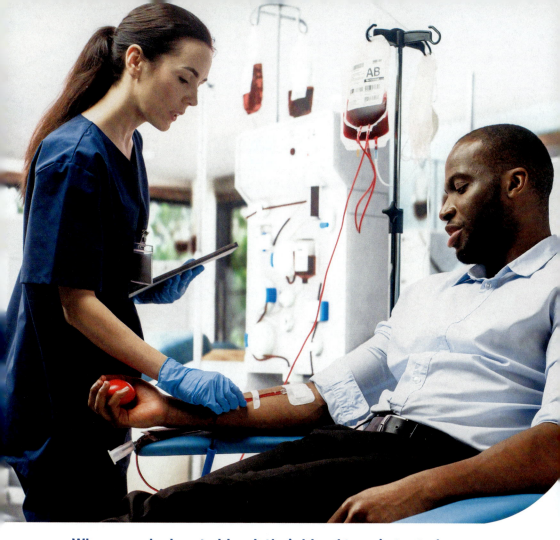

When people donate blood, their blood type is tested. People can also learn their blood type by asking a doctor for a test.

There are more than 600 known blood antigens. But the most important are called A and B. Someone may have only one of these antigens on their blood cells. They would have type A or type B blood.

Another person may have both antigens. They would have type AB blood. And some people have neither antigen. They have type O blood.

A protein called Rh factor also indicates blood type. This antigen is either present or absent. If it is present, the blood is positive. If it is absent, the blood is negative. Combinations of these antigens result in eight main blood types. The most common blood type in the United States is O positive. The least common is AB negative.

BLOOD VESSELS

Blood travels through blood vessels. Blood vessels extend throughout the body. They vary in size. The aorta is the largest.

The average adult has about 60,000 miles (100,000 km) of blood vessels.

This artery brings blood from the heart to the rest of the body. It is 1 inch (2.5 cm) wide. Other blood vessels are so thin that only a single red blood cell can pass through at a time.

Blood vessels fall into three types. These types are arteries, veins, and capillaries.

Arteries carry blood away from the heart. They typically transport oxygen-rich blood. Veins carry blood toward the heart. The blood in veins is usually low in oxygen. Capillaries connect arteries and veins.

Capillaries are the smallest blood vessels. However, they are very important. Oxygen and nutrients enter cells through capillaries. These vessels have thin walls. Substances pass through the walls and into nearby cells. Similarly, carbon dioxide and waste enter the blood at the capillaries.

THE HEART

The heart is the main organ of the circulatory system. It sits slightly to the left within the chest. The heart squeezes to

THE HUMAN HEART

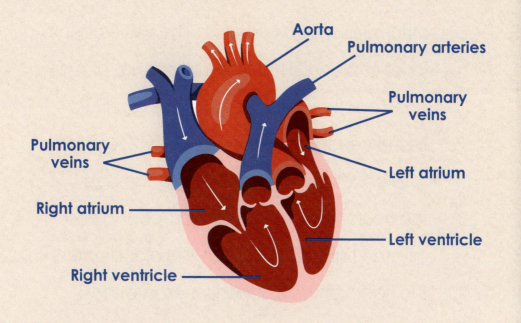

This diagram displays the parts of the heart and how blood flows through them.

push blood through the blood vessels. Special cells within the heart control how fast it beats.

The heart has four chambers. The upper chambers are the left and right atria. The lower chambers are the left and right ventricles. A valve separates each atrium from the ventricles. The valve opens to let in blood. Then it shuts so that blood does not flow backward. A thick wall of tissue separates the left and right ventricles.

Blood flows in one direction through the heart. Veins carry oxygen-poor blood into the right atrium. Then the blood enters the right ventricle. It continues into the pulmonary arteries. These are the only arteries that carry oxygen-poor blood. They connect the heart to the lungs. The blood picks up oxygen in the lungs. The pulmonary veins then carry the oxygen-rich blood back to the heart. These are the only veins in the body that carry oxygen-rich blood.

Blood from the pulmonary veins enters the left atrium. It moves into the left ventricle. From there, the blood flows into the aorta. Many arteries branch from the aorta. These arteries carry oxygen-rich blood throughout the body.

Doctors can listen to a patient's heart by using a tool called a stethoscope. Some heart conditions can cause the heart to produce abnormal sounds.

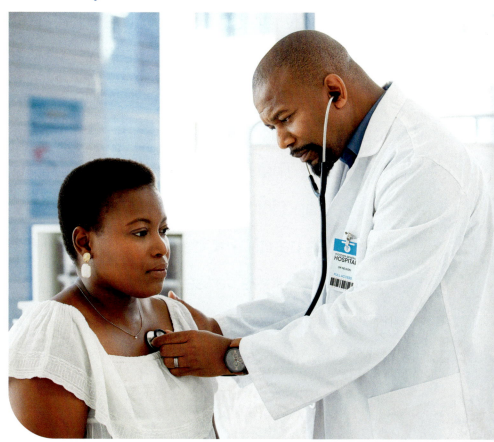

CHAPTER THREE

WHAT CAN GO WRONG WITH THE CIRCULATORY SYSTEM?

The body relies on the circulatory system for a constant supply of oxygen and nutrients. Problems with the heart, blood, and blood vessels can disrupt this supply. That means that circulatory diseases and injuries can seriously affect a person's health. Professor Mark Kearney says, "If the blood vessels aren't working very well, it affects everything."[3]

To become cardiologists, doctors train for at least 3 years in addition to their general medical training.

Many circulatory conditions share the same risk factors. Risk factors raise the likelihood of developing a disease. For example, old age is a risk factor for heart disease. But people of any age can develop circulatory conditions.

CONDITIONS OF THE HEART

Heart attacks are among the most serious conditions of the heart. Heart attacks occur when blood flow to the heart is blocked. A buildup of plaque can block blood flow in arteries. Plaque is a mixture of fat and **cholesterol**. Blood clots can also interrupt blood flow.

Coronary artery disease (CAD) occurs when plaque builds up in blood vessels that lead to the heart. CAD raises the risk of

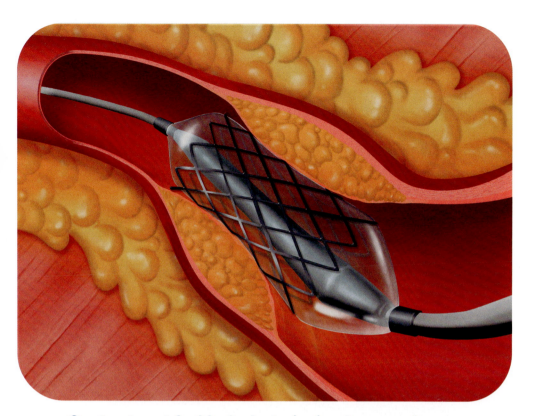

One treatment for blocked arteries involves opening up the artery with an expandable metal tube called a stent.

heart attacks. Many people do not realize they have CAD until a heart attack occurs. CAD is extremely common. About 18 million US adults have CAD. It is the leading cause of death worldwide.

High blood pressure is a risk factor of heart disease. Blood pressure describes how much force is needed to push blood through the arteries. The heart works harder when blood pressure is high. This can raise the risk of heart disease and heart attacks. Many things can cause high

People can measure their blood pressure using a device called a blood pressure cuff.

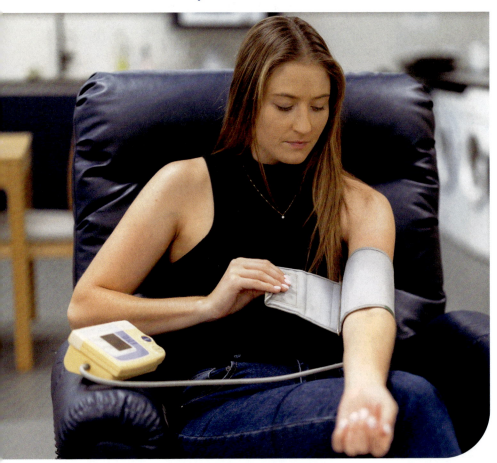

blood pressure. A buildup of plaque that narrows arteries can raise blood pressure. Lack of exercise can cause high blood pressure as well.

Chest pain is the most common symptom of a heart attack. But some people do not report this discomfort. Other symptoms include nausea and shortness of breath. Some people break out in a cold sweat during a heart attack.

A heart attack is different from heart failure. Heart attacks occur when blood flow is suddenly interrupted. Heart failure happens slowly. The heart weakens over time. It becomes unable to pump blood efficiently.

Some heart conditions are present at birth. People can be born with

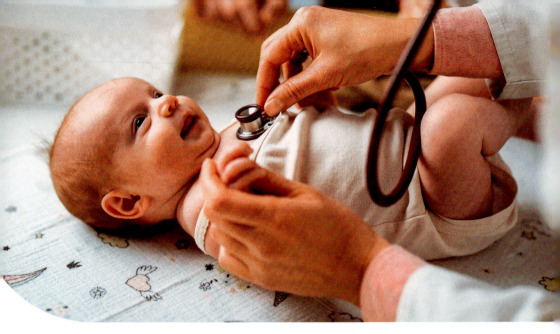

Conditions present at birth are called congenital conditions.

heart defects. These conditions affect the structure of the heart. They can cause issues with blood flow. This can put strain on the heart.

There are many types of heart defects. Sometimes valves do not work properly. Other defects cause a hole to form between chambers. Oxygen-rich and oxygen-poor blood may mix together. This results in reduced oxygen delivery.

Heart defects can be deadly. But treatment has improved over time. About 90 percent of infants with heart defects survive into adulthood following treatment. Surgery is the most common treatment for heart defects.

CONDITIONS OF THE BLOOD

Sickle cell anemia (SCA) is a blood disorder that is present at birth. It is the most common inherited blood disorder in the United States. Approximately 2,000 babies are diagnosed with SCA each year. SCA affects red blood cells. Red blood cells are typically flexible and shaped like discs. But they are misshapen in people with SCA. They are fragile and c shaped.

They stick together easily. This can block blood vessels.

SCA causes tiredness and pain. Other symptoms include shortness of breath and a rapid heart rate. Stress and not getting enough water can worsen symptoms.

SCA used to be fatal before adulthood in most cases. But treatments now allow about half of people with SCA to live into their 50s. Medication helps people manage SCA. People can also avoid situations that make their symptoms worse. Sydney is a young adult living with SCA. She has learned to manage her disease. She says, "Many people still think that [SCA] is a death sentence. But having this disease is not a death sentence."[4]

Leukemia is a type of cancer. It affects blood production. Leukemia causes the body to produce a large amount of

Radiation therapy is sometimes used as part of the treatment for leukemia. This treatment involves a machine that kills cancer cells using powerful waves of energy.

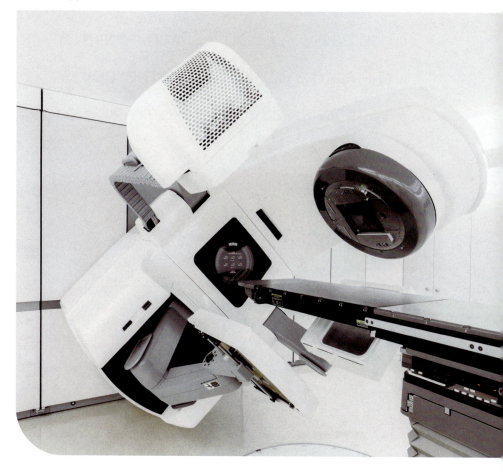

abnormal blood cells. These blood cells do not work properly.

Leukemia has many symptoms. It can cause fevers. It can also cause chills. People with leukemia may report bone pain. They may feel tired often. They may bleed easily. A blood test can confirm a leukemia diagnosis. **Chemotherapy** is a common treatment for leukemia.

Hemophilia

Hemophilia is a rare **genetic** disorder. It affects blood clotting. Platelets work together with special proteins to stop bleeding. People with this condition have low levels of these proteins. They are unable to form clots quickly. They may bleed for a long time after a minor injury. They are also at higher risk for internal bleeding.

CONDITIONS OF THE BLOOD VESSELS

Damage to the blood vessels can cause bleeding. Losing too much blood can be fatal. Bleeding can be external or internal. External bleeding is visible. For example, a cut on the skin causes blood to flow to the surface. This is external bleeding. Internal bleeding happens inside the body. It may not be as obvious as external bleeding. Pain and tightness at the site of injury can be a sign of internal bleeding. People may become nauseous. They may fall unconscious.

Severe bleeding can be deadly. Organs can begin to fail if blood loss is not treated. Blood transfusions are used to treat severe bleeding. This treatment involves giving

Collected blood can be stored and transported in plastic blood bags. These bags can also be used during blood transfusions.

patients blood from donors. The blood is injected into a patient's blood vessels. It then begins to work for the patient.

Blood types matter in blood transfusions. People cannot receive blood that has a foreign antigen. For example, a person with type A blood cannot receive type B blood. A person who is Rh negative cannot receive Rh positive blood. People who are O negative lack these antigens. They can receive only O negative blood. But they are universal donors. That means anyone can receive the blood they donate. People who are AB positive have all these antigens. They are universal recipients. They can receive blood of any type.

Strokes are life-threatening conditions. They occur when blood flow to the brain is blocked. This prevents the brain from receiving oxygen. Blood clots in an artery leading to the brain can cause strokes. Aneurysms can also cause strokes. An aneurysm occurs when the wall of an artery weakens. The artery may widen as blood flows through it. Eventually, the artery may burst.

Heart attacks and strokes are medical emergencies and require immediate treatment. Emergency telephone numbers are one way for people to get help.

Strokes can happen suddenly. It is important to know their signs. Confusion is a common sign of strokes. A person having a stroke may have trouble following a conversation. Strokes can also cause numbness or weakness on one side of the body. For example, one side of the mouth may droop. Or the left arm and leg may become weak. A sudden change in vision is another symptom.

Barrie Gough had a stroke when he was 59 years old. He talked about his symptoms. "I didn't experience any kind of pain, just a strange feeling," he said. "I mentioned it to my wife, who went to get me a drink, and realized I had lost the use of my right arm."[5]

WHAT CAN HUMANS DO TO KEEP THE CIRCULATORY SYSTEM HEALTHY?

People can adopt habits to improve circulatory health. A healthy diet helps prevent heart disease. So does regular exercise. Managing stress also benefits the circulatory system.

A healthy diet can lower blood pressure. It can also reduce cholesterol levels. Dr. Kaveh Bookani talks about the importance of a heart-healthy diet. "By prioritizing healthy eating, individuals can

There is no one correct healthy diet. Doctors work with their patients to create eating plans that work best for them.

reduce their risk of heart disease," he says. "This includes choosing nutritious foods and avoiding unhealthy fats and excessive sodium."[6]

Vegetables are central to many healthy diets. Whole grains can also be a part of a healthy diet. People also need to eat foods containing protein. Protein-rich foods include lean meat and fish. Eggs, nuts, and beans are also heart-healthy sources of protein.

A poor diet can harm the circulatory system. People should limit the amount of salt they eat. High levels of salt in the blood increase blood pressure. Too much saturated fat can also be unhealthy. Butter, cheese, and fatty meats contain lots of saturated fats. Saturated fats raise

Nutrition Facts

1 serving per container
Serving size   1 package (97g)

Amount per serving

Calories   **270**

% Daily Value*

Total Fat 22g	**28%**
Saturated Fat 7g	**35%**
Trans Fat 0g	
Cholesterol 95mg	**32%**
Sodium 1060mg	**46%**
Total Carbohydrate 8g	**3%**
Dietary Fiber 0g	**0%**
Total Sugars 0g	
Includes 0g Added Sugars	**0%**
Protein 11g	**16%**
Vitamin D 0mcg	0%
Calcium 120mg	10%
Iron 2mg	10%
Potassium 100mg	2%

* The % Daily Value (DV) tells you how much a nutrient in a serving of food contributes to a daily diet. 2,000 calories a day is used for general nutrition advice.

INGREDIENTS: POTTED MEAT MADE WITH CHICKEN, PORK ADDED (MECHANICALLY SEPARATED CHICKEN, PORK, WATER, SALT, CONTAINS 2% OR LESS OF: MUSTARD, VINEGAR, DEXTROSE, SODIUM ERYTHORBATE, GARLIC POWDER, NATURAL FLAVORS, SODIUM NITRITE). CRACKERS (WHEAT FLOUR,

Most packaged food in the United States must be sold with a nutrition facts label. People can read these labels to see what kinds of nutrients and ingredients the food contains.

cholesterol levels. This can increase the risk of heart disease and strokes. Unsaturated fats, such as vegetable oils, are healthier. Limiting sugars is another way to improve health. Eating too much sugar is linked to high blood pressure and heart disease.

Intense exercise temporarily raises one's heart rate. This strengthens heart muscles.

EXERCISE

Exercise has many benefits for the circulatory system. It improves circulation. It also strengthens the heart. Consistent exercise lowers one's resting heart rate. This means the heart does not have to work as hard when the body is at rest.

Dr. Ross Brown talks about the importance of regular exercise. "We know it helps control a lot of risk factors, such as . . . blood pressure," he says. "If arteries aren't challenged with changes in blood flow, it makes them stiff and more prone to issues."[7]

Medical experts recommend getting 2.5 hours of exercise each week. Intense and frequent workouts benefit the

Aerobic Exercise

Aerobic exercise is exercise that raises a person's heart rate and breathing. It is usually practiced for an extended period of time. Walking, jogging, and swimming are examples of aerobic exercise. Aerobic exercise helps improve circulatory health. It can lower blood pressure and reduce cholesterol.

circulatory system the most. But some activity is better than none. Walking, gardening, and taking the stairs all improve circulation. Starting with less intense activities can help people build up to more intense workouts.

REDUCING STRESS

Stress affects physical and mental health. It is harmful to the circulatory system. Stress can raise heart rate and blood pressure. It can even raise the risk of heart attacks. Managing stress can improve circulatory health.

Research shows that practicing mindfulness can lower stress. Mindfulness is the practice of paying attention to the present. People may do this by focusing on

Breathing exercises can help people practice mindfulness. These exercises often involve breathing slowly and regularly.

Exercising with others can help people stay committed to an exercise routine.

their breathing. They may also concentrate on their senses.

Social activities can help reduce stress. Loved ones can offer support during stressful times. But taking time for oneself can also be helpful. This might include engaging in a hobby. It can also mean taking time to relax.

The circulatory system is essential to human life. It delivers oxygen and nutrients throughout the body. It helps defend against disease and infection. Issues with the circulatory system can have a big impact on people's lives. That means it's important to take steps to keep the circulatory system healthy.

GLOSSARY

cardiologist

a doctor who diagnoses and treats conditions that affect the circulatory system

chemotherapy

a treatment for cancer that involves using anti-cancer medications

cholesterol

a fat-like substance that the body uses in many ways

genetic

relating to genes, the information passed from parents to their offspring that determines traits such as hair color

germs

very small bacteria, fungi, viruses, or similar organisms that can cause disease

glands

body parts that release substances such as saliva

organs

structures of body tissues that work together to perform specific functions

respiratory

relating to breathing

SOURCE NOTES

CHAPTER ONE: WHAT IS THE CIRCULATORY SYSTEM?

1. Quoted in Tanya Lewis and Scott Dutfield, "Human Heart: Anatomy, Function & Facts," *Live Science*, July 27, 2022. www.livescience.com.

CHAPTER TWO: HOW DOES THE CIRCULATORY SYSTEM WORK?

2. Marlene Stephanie Williams, MD, "What Are Platelets and Why Are They Important?," *Johns Hopkins Medicine*, n.d. www.hopkinsmedicine.org.

CHAPTER THREE: WHAT CAN GO WRONG WITH THE CIRCULATORY SYSTEM?

3. Quoted in "How Your Blood Supply Connects Everything," *British Heart Foundation*, n.d. www.bhf.org.uk.

4. Quoted in "How Two Sisters Continue to Soar with Sickle Cell Disease," *UNC School of Medicine*, February 2, 2024. https://news.unchealthcare.org.

5. Quoted in "How Your Blood Supply Connects Everything."

CHAPTER FOUR: WHAT CAN HUMANS DO TO KEEP THE CIRCULATORY SYSTEM HEALTHY?

6. Quoted in "What Does a Heart-Healthy Diet Look Like?," *Nebraska Medicine*, May 2, 2024. www.nebraskamed.com.

7. Quoted in Virginia Pelley, "How to Improve Circulation and Blood Flow, According to Experts," *Forbes Health*, February 15, 2024. www.forbes.com.

FOR FURTHER RESEARCH

BOOKS

Jonas Edwards, *The Circulatory System*. New York:
    Gareth Stevens, 2021.

Tammy Gagne, *The Human Respiratory System*. San Diego, CA:
    BrightPoint Press, 2025.

Yvette LaPierre, *Handling Sickle Cell Disease*. Minneapolis, MN:
    Abdo, 2022.

INTERNET SOURCES

"Heart-Healthy Living," *National Heart, Lung, and Blood Institute*,
    April 23, 2024. www.nhlbi.nih.gov.

"Living with Congenital Heart Disease," *Heart Matters (blog), British Heart
    Foundation*, June 2023. www.bhf.org.uk.

"Strategies to Prevent Heart Disease," *Mayo Clinic*, August 17, 2023.
    www.mayoclinic.org.

WEBSITES

American Red Cross
www.redcross.org

The American Red Cross responds to disasters and provides medical aid to people in need. Drives to collect blood donations are one way the Red Cross provides aid. The organization hosts blood drives across the United States.

Leukemia and Lymphoma Society (LLS)
www.lls.org

The LLS is a nonprofit organization that is dedicated to finding cures for leukemia and similar diseases. People can visit its website to learn more about leukemia symptoms and treatment.

Sickle Cell Disease Association of America
www.sicklecelldisease.org

The Sickle Cell Disease Association of America works toward finding a cure for sickle cell anemia. It aims to raise awareness about the disease.

INDEX

IMAGE CREDITS

ABOUT THE AUTHOR

Chelsea Xie lives in San Diego, California. She solves crossword puzzles and swims to keep her mind and body healthy.